IMAGES OF GOD

IMAGES OF GOD

BY JOHN AND KATHERINE PATERSON
ILLUSTRATED BY ALEXANDER KOSHKIN

CLARION BOOKS
New York

Clarion Books
a Houghton Mifflin Company imprint
215 Park Avenue South, New York, NY 10003
Text copyright © 1998 by Minna Murra, Inc.
Illustrations copyright © 1998 by Alexander Koshkin
Illustrations executed in watercolor, tempera, and gouache
Text is 14/18-point Dante
Book design by Carol Goldenberg

Printed in Singapore.

Library of Congress Cataloging-in-Publication Data

Paterson, John (John Barstow)
Images of God / by John and Katherine Paterson.
p.   cm.
Summary: Explores some of the images which biblical writers use to teach about God;
images include light, rock, and wind as well as a gardener, father, and architect.
ISBN: 0-395-70734-X
1. God—Biblical teaching—Juvenile literature. 2. Symbolism in the Bible—Juvenile lit-
erature. [1. God. 2. Symbolism in the Bible.] I. Paterson, Katherine. II. Title.
BS544.P37 1998
231—dc21   97-21637
CIP   AC
TWP 10 9 8 7 6 5 4 3 2 1

For Ted and Alice Vial,
in whom we see the Invisible,
with gratitude and love

CONTENTS

In No Strange Land

"The Kingdom of God is within you"

O world invisible, we view thee,
O world intangible, we touch thee,
O world unknowable, we know thee,
Inapprehensible, we clutch thee!

Does the fish soar to find the ocean,
The eagle plunge to find the air—
That we ask of the stars in motion
If they have rumor of thee there?

Not where the wheeling systems darken,
And our benumbed conceiving soars!—
The drift of pinions, would we hearken,
Beats at our own clay-shuttered doors.

The angels keep their ancient places;—
Turn but a stone, and start a wing!
'Tis ye, 'tis your estranged faces,
That miss the many-splendored thing.

But (when so sad thou canst not sadder)
Cry—and upon thy so sore loss
Shall shine the traffic of Jacob's ladder
Pitched betwixt Heaven and Charing Cross.

Yea, in the night, my Soul, my daughter,
Cry—clinging Heaven by the hems;
And lo, Christ walking on the water
Not of Gennesareth, but Thames!

Francis Thompson
(1859–1907)

INTRODUCTION

How do you see the invisible? How do you touch the spiritual? How do you know that which is far beyond human knowledge? How do you grasp what cannot be apprehended? The poet Francis Thompson says that our problem lies in us—that the invisible world is very near, that the wings of angels beat upon our hearts, but we fail to pay attention.

> 'Tis ye, 'tis your estranged faces,
> That miss the many-splendored thing.

But how can we imagine God without making God in our own image? Those of us in the Judeo-Christian tradition share with our Muslim brothers and sisters a nervousness about images of God. God cannot be reduced to an idol that can be seen and handled, and people who think they know God fully have mistaken the Eternal for an idol they have made with their own minds. None of us can see God whole, but we can, if the Bible is to be believed, have glimpses of the Almighty.

The Bible is full of these word pictures; even the Christian doctrine of the Trinity is a word picture—God as Father, God as Son, God as Spirit, three aspects of the One who cannot be divided or defined.

This is a book about some of the images that the Biblical writers use to help us know more about God: who God is, what God is like. No image will teach us all there is to know about God, of course, nor will the sum of all the images. What we know of God is what God chooses to reveal to people. God's revelation comes to human beings in the situations of their lives.

What is God like? The shepherd tending his sheep says God is like a loving shepherd. A person who lives in a monarchy says God is like a great and powerful king. A desert dweller says God is like a shadow of a huge rock where one can take refuge from the sun. The images that the Biblical writers use are images that would have been very familiar to the people of their times. Some, like shepherd or king, are not images that mean as much to people of our place or time, but others of these images—light and rock and wind—are as familiar to us as they were to ancient peoples.

As we explore these images with words, Alexander Koshkin will explore them in art. Mr. Koshkin is Russian and has waited many years for the freedom to paint Biblical themes. It gives us great joy to be able to work with him in the creation of this book. *John and Katherine Paterson*

Note: A word of explanation about the "Bible." For Jews the Bible consists of thirty-nine books. The first five of these are called the Torah, or the Law, and are the most important for Jews. The other thirty-four books contain historical writings, the words and lives of the prophets, and assorted "wisdom literature" such as Psalms and Proverbs. This was the Bible that Jesus and his disciples knew and often quoted. The Christian Bible contains these thirty-nine books and calls them the Old Testament or Old Covenant. In addition to the Hebrew Bible, Christian leaders in the fourth century A.D. declared twenty-seven Christian writings as Canon. That meant that from that time on, Christians should regard these books, along with the Hebrew Bible, as the church's standard for faith and behavior, making a *total* of sixty-six books in the Christian Bible. The first four (the Gospels) tell of the life of Jesus; one (the Acts) tells of the founding of the Christian church. The other twenty-two books are letters from early church leaders to the Christian congregations scattered about the Roman Empire. The New Testament does not replace the Hebrew Bible. In fact, Jesus and his twelve initial disciples were all devout Jews and saw their ministry as a fulfillment of the prophecies of the Hebrew scriptures. That is why in this book we have tried to show the dependence of the New Testament upon the Hebrew Bible and the interconnection of the two.

In this book the translation of the Bible most commonly cited will be The New Revised Standard Version, Thomas Nelson Publishers © 1989. Occasionally we will combine several translations or paraphrase for the sake of clarity.

ALL NATURE SINGS

Images from the Created World

LIGHT

In the Bible, God's first words are: "Let there be light." For the Biblical writers light was so basic to life that they often used it as an image for the God who made it. The writer of Psalm 27 declared: "The Lord is my light and my salvation; whom shall I fear?"

Light takes many different forms. Think of the rainbow. All its varied colors come from the light of the sun reaching us through particles of water. In the same way the light of God's presence shines through the experiences of our lives—sometimes bright yellow, sometimes a darkened blue, sometimes a mysterious purple. When the Biblical writers speak of "the glory of God," they are picturing a radiance that indicates God's presence. When we give glory to God, we reflect in praise and adoration the One True Light of the world.

In the Book of Revelation the writer paints a scene of a heavenly city, the new Jerusalem, where "there will be no more night; they need no light of lamp or sun, for the Lord God will be their light." [Revelation 22:5]

The religious people of Jesus' time must have been shocked when Jesus said: "I am the light of the world." But Jesus also said to his disciples: "You are the light of the world," indicating that just as the moon reflects the sun's light, so we who love God are meant to reflect God's love to the world.

The Apostle Paul took Jesus' words seriously in his letter to the Corinthian Church. "It is the God who said, 'Let light shine out of darkness,' who has shone in our hearts to give the light of the knowledge of the glory of God in the face of Jesus Christ." [II Corinthians 4:6]

Light is both an idea and an experience, giving rainbow variations to our relationship with God.

WATER

As a deer longs for flowing streams,
so my soul longs for you, O God.
My soul thirsts for God,
for the living God.

[Psalm 42:1–2]

One day Jesus and his disciples were traveling from Judea to Galilee, and they passed through the region of Samaria. Now in those days Jews did not like to travel through Samaria—some even took the long way around to keep from walking through the area. This hatred between the Jews and the Samaritans dated back seven hundred years. The Assyrians had conquered the Kingdom of Israel and taken many of its people into captivity. The remaining Israelites intermarried with the colonists that the Assyrians imported to repopulate the area of Samaria. The people of Samaria were therefore of mixed national and religious heritage, and most of the Jews looked down on them.

Jesus was resting by Jacob's well when a woman came out of the city to fill her water jar. He asked the woman to give him a drink of water.

The woman was astonished. Here was a man—a Jew she was sure—asking her, a Samaritan woman, for a favor. Usually Jews and Samaritans didn't even speak, much less share a drinking cup. "How is it," she asked, "that you, a Jew, ask me for a drink?"

"If you knew who was speaking to you," Jesus answered, "you'd ask and he'd give you living water."

"What are you talking about?" the woman said. "This well is deep, and you don't even have a bucket. Where will you get this living water? Are you greater than Jacob, our ancestor who gave us this well a thousand years ago?"

"People who drink from this well will soon be thirsty again," Jesus said, "but those who drink of the water I give will never be thirsty. That water will become in them like a spring of water gushing up to eternal life."

"All right," said the woman. "Give me some of your water so I'll never be thirsty, much less have to come back day after day to draw water from this well."

"Go call your husband and come back here with him."

"I don't have a husband," the woman said.

"No," Jesus agreed, "you don't have a husband. You've had five husbands, and the man you are living with now is not your husband."

Once again the woman was astonished. How could this

stranger know so much about her? She quickly shifted the sub-
ject off her personal affairs to the religious argument that the
Jews had carried on with the Samaritans for hundreds of years.
"I see you're a prophet," she said. "Our ancestors worshipped
God on this mountain, but you Jews say that God must be
worshipped in Jerusalem. Which of us is right?"

"The time will come," Jesus said, "when people will worship
neither on this mountain nor in Jerusalem. God is spirit, and
those who worship God must worship in spirit and in truth."

"The Messiah, God's Chosen One, is coming," the woman
said. "When he comes, he'll explain everything to us."

Jesus said to her, "I am he. The one who is speaking to you now."

Just then Jesus' disciples returned. They were amazed to find Jesus, a Jewish teacher, speaking to a common Samaritan woman, but they didn't dare ask questions. The woman herself hurried back to the city, leaving her water jar behind. She said to everyone she saw, "Come see a man who told me all about myself. Can he be the Messiah?"

Many Samaritans came out to the well to see this prophet. Jesus stayed in the area for two days talking with those who came, after which the other Samaritans said to the woman, "It's no longer because of what you said that we believe. Now we have heard for ourselves, and we have come to know that this is truly the Savior of the world." [Retold from John 4:3–42]

Be appalled, O heavens, at this,
    be shocked, be utterly desolate, says the Lord,
for my people have committed two evils:
    they have forsaken me,
the fountain of living water,
    and dug out cisterns for themselves,
cracked cisterns
    that can hold no water.

[Jeremiah 2:12–13]

In a dry land, water becomes very precious. So we often find the Biblical writers thinking of God as the cool, life-giving refreshment of streams in the desert. Water is one of the most frequently mentioned realities in the Bible. From the story of creation in the book of Genesis to the story of the new creation in the book of Revelation, water plays a major role. "A wind [or spirit] from God swept over the face of the waters," says the writer of Genesis as he paints the picture of the act of creating the world. [Genesis 1:2] And in the final scenes described in the book of Revelation, the writer says:

> Then the angel showed me the river of the water of life, bright as crystal, flowing from the throne of God and of the Lamb through the middle of the street of the city. . . .

> *The Spirit and the bride say,*
> *"Come."*
> *And let everyone who hears say,*
> *"Come."*
> *And let everyone who is thirsty come.*
> *Let anyone who wishes take the water of life as a gift.*
> [Revelation 22:1–2,17]

WIND

Nicodemus was a Pharisee, a devout Jew, and a leader of his people. When he heard about the carpenter of Nazareth who was going about the countryside teaching about the Kingdom of God, he was curious.

Who was this Jesus who preached to the poor and healed the sick? Was he a disciple of the devil, as some said? Nicodemus did not think so. How could a man in league with the devil go about the countryside making the blind see and the lame walk? He must be like one of the prophets of old times. But Jesus didn't act like Jeremiah or Ezekiel. He didn't preach thundering sermons against the wickedness of the people. Rather, he told them stories.

Jesus claimed to be a practicing Jew, but he was not careful of the holy laws. He did his work of healing on the Sabbath, when a religious person should be resting. He went to the homes of tax collectors and ate and drank with them. No proper Jew would make friends with people who worked for the hated

Roman conquerors. Neither would a devout Jew be seen in the company of prostitutes and other known sinners.

Nicodemus determined to find out for himself what kind of man this Jesus was. But Nicodemus was a very important person. He was a member of the Sanhedrin, the highest ruling council of the Jews. If he went to hear Jesus preach, rumors might start that he was becoming one of Jesus' followers. He couldn't risk that.

He found out where Jesus was staying, and one night, after the streets had emptied, he secretly made his way to the place and asked to see the young teacher.

"Rabbi," Nicodemus said politely, when the two of them were alone, "I know you are a teacher sent from God, for I don't see how anyone could do what you do unless God were with him." He was about to go on and ask Jesus the questions he had on his mind when Jesus said something very peculiar.

"I will tell you the truth," Jesus said. "No one can see the Kingdom of God unless he is born again."

Nicodemus hadn't even planned to ask about the Kingdom of God. He'd planned to talk about Jesus himself, so he was a bit startled to get an answer for which he hadn't asked any question. Besides, the answer didn't make any sense. What did this young teacher mean? He was annoyed. "How can anyone be born after he's grown?" he asked. "Can he get inside his mother's womb a second time and be born all over again?"

But Jesus wasn't talking about that kind of birth. "What I'm saying," replied Jesus, "is that no one can enter the Kingdom of

God who isn't born of water and Spirit. You are talking about being born of the flesh. What is born of the flesh is flesh and what is born of the Spirit is spirit. You shouldn't be surprised when I say that you must be born in a new way. It is like the wind that blows wherever it chooses. You can hear the sound of the wind, but you don't know where it comes from or where it goes. It is the same way with a person who is born of the Spirit of God."

"I don't understand what you're talking about," Nicodemus answered. "How can this be?"

"As I have been going about preaching to the people, I have been bearing testimony to what I know about God's work in the world, but you and your fellow Pharisees haven't accepted what I have said. If I've told you about earthly things and you haven't believed me, how can I tell you about heavenly things?"

And then the young teacher reminded Nicodemus of a story about Moses. "Do you remember when the Israelites disobeyed God in the wilderness and many of them were bitten by poisonous serpents?"

Of course, Nicodemus knew all the stories of his people.

"God commanded Moses to make a bronze serpent and lift it up so that all the people who looked at it might live [Numbers 21:9]. In the same way," Jesus said, "the Son of Man must be lifted up, that whoever believes in him may have life eternal."

While Nicodemus knew that when the Scriptures used the term "the Son of Man," they meant the Messiah, he did not know what Jesus meant by the Son of Man being "lifted up."

"God has loved the world so much," Jesus continued, "that he gave his only son that everyone who believes in him will not know destruction but will have eternal life."

Nicodemus did not become a disciple of Jesus that night; indeed, he told no one that he had visited with Jesus, but he could not forget that midnight conversation. Later, when his fellow Pharisees of the Sanhedrin were seeking to arrest Jesus for blasphemy, Nicodemus objected. "It is against our law to judge a person without first giving him a hearing to let him say for himself what he is doing," he said to them.

The others turned on Nicodemus scornfully, so he said no more, but when Jesus was crucified—lifted up on the cross— Nicodemus was at last moved to action. Joseph of Arimathea, another secret disciple, went to the Roman authorities and asked permission to take away the body of Jesus. Nicodemus also came, the Gospel of John tells us, bringing about a hundred pounds of precious spices. The two of them wrapped Jesus' body with the myrrh and aloes in linen cloths, according to the Jewish custom of the time, and laid the body in a tomb in Joseph's garden.

[Retold from John 3:1–21; 7:51–52; and 19:38–42]

In some ways, although Nicodemus seemed puzzled by it, wind is a particularly fitting image for God, for although we can't see the wind itself, we are very conscious of its power as we watch it bend the trees or push a sailboat across a lake. In the Hebrew Bible the same Hebrew word *ruach* means wind, breath, and spirit. Similarly, in the Greek New Testament the word *pneuma* can mean all three. In the first chapter of Genesis the translators of the King James Version of the Bible said that "the Spirit of God moved upon the face of the waters." In the New Revised Standard Version, we are told that "a wind from God swept over the face of the waters." But this is the same word that is used in describing the creation of Adam in chapter two, where the writer says that "the Lord God formed man from the dust of the ground, and *breathed* into his nostrils the *breath* of life; and the man became a living being." In the Greek New Testament when Jesus is talking to the skeptical Nicodemus about being born in a new way, the writer uses the various meanings of *pneuma* much as the writer of Genesis used *ruach*.

God is Spirit. God is the mysterious breath of life. God is the power that moves the forces of nature and works invisibly in the human heart.

FIRE

As he wandered about in the wilderness of Midian, taking care of his father-in-law's sheep, Moses thought often of his wasted life. His parents, like all the Israelites in Egypt, were slaves. His people had come to Egypt many years before, when his ancestor Joseph had been prime minister to the Pharaoh, or king of Egypt. But before many years passed, the Egyptians forgot about Joseph and how he had saved their land and many of the surrounding peoples from famine.

During Joseph's time as prime minister, his brothers, the other sons of Jacob, had come down to Egypt searching for food. They were surprised and frightened to learn that the prime minister was the same little brother whom they had sold into slavery years before. Joseph forgave his brothers for the evil they had done him. "God meant your evil for good," he said and persuaded them to bring his father and all the rest of the great extended family to live in Egypt under his protection.

The years went by and the Israelites grew in number and strength until they became a threat to their host country. The

Pharaoh set them to work building supply cities. Even as slaves the Israelites (or Hebrews, as they were also called) prospered and grew more and more numerous, so the Pharaoh of that day decided that all the male children must be killed.

When Moses was born, his mother could not bear the thought that he might be killed, so she wove a papyrus basket and made it waterproof with bitumen and pitch and set it in the reeds by the riverbank. She left Moses' sister Miriam to watch over her brother.

Before long the Pharaoh's daughter came down to the river to bathe. She found the infant Moses and decided to adopt him. At Miriam's suggestion, she hired Moses' own mother to take care of him in his early years, until he was ready to come to the palace and be educated as a prince of Egypt should be.

Surely Moses was destined for a life as marvelous as that of Joseph before him. Then one day, walking about the construction sites, he saw an Egyptian overseer beating a Hebrew slave. Moses was enraged and, thinking no one was about, he killed the Egyptian and hid his body in the sand.

The next day he saw two Hebrews fighting with each other and when he tried to intervene, one of them said to him, "Who made you a prince and judge over us? Are you planning to kill me the way you killed that Egyptian yesterday?" Moses was terrified to realize that his crime was known. He fled into the wilderness before word of it could reach Pharaoh.

He had lived in the wilderness for a long time now, married to the daughter of a wandering desert priest. But he was still homesick—if not for the palace of the Pharaoh then for his enslaved people. He had meant to use his position to help them, as Joseph had helped them long before, but in a fit of rage he had killed that possibility just as he had killed the offending Egyptian. He named the son, born to him in the wilderness, Gershom, which meant "A stranger here," for, he said, "I have been a stranger in a strange land."

Now in search of food and water for the sheep, he had wandered beyond Midian to the slope of a mountain. There on the mountainside he saw a strange sight. It was a bush, ablaze with fire, but somehow the leaves and branches were not burning up.

Curious, Moses went closer to this strange sight, and as he did, he heard a voice calling to him from the middle of the fiery bush.

"Moses, Moses."

"Here I am," he answered.

"Don't come any closer," the voice said. "And take off your sandals. For you are standing on holy ground."

Moses was very frightened. What could be the meaning of this vision?

"I am the God of Abraham, the God of Isaac, and the God of Jacob," the voice continued. Now Moses covered his face, for the Hebrews believed that no one could look at God and live to tell of it.

"I have seen how miserable my people are," God said. "I have seen how the Egyptians oppress them. I am going to deliver them from Pharaoh and bring them into a new land, a

land so rich that it seems to flow with milk and honey. And you are the one I have chosen to send to Pharaoh to bring my people out of slavery."

Moses was filled with terror. How could he, a murderer on the run, return to the court of the Pharaoh? "Who am I," he asked, "to go before Pharaoh and lead the Israelites out of Egypt?"

"I will be with you," God answered. "And I promise you that you and the people will worship me right here on this holy mountain."

But Moses was still frightened. In their long years of suffering, the people were sure that the God of Abraham, Isaac, and Jacob had forgotten about them. At any rate, there weren't many left who had much faith that the God of olden times would be of any help to them, if they believed that God existed at all. "If I go down there and say to the people that the God of their fathers has sent me to lead them, they're sure to ask me what your name is. What am I supposed to say then?" Moses asked.

Now in those days, the name of a person or a god was very important. The name stood for the person's whole being. If you knew someone's name, you had a certain power over him. Perhaps Moses figured that God would not tell him the true name and Moses would be spared this dangerous assignment.

But the voice answered, giving Moses a name that was not a proper noun but a form of the verb *to be* which could be understood to mean "I am who I am" or "I will be what I will be." "Tell them," the voice said, "I AM has sent you to them."

Now you might imagine that when God gave Moses this powerful new name that no one had ever heard before, Moses would have immediately agreed to do what God asked, but Moses kept arguing and making excuses. First, he said that the people might not believe that God had sent him. In reply to this, God gave Moses some signs or miracles he could perform for those who demanded proofs. The shepherd's stick that Moses carried turned into a snake and then back into an ordinary stick. If Moses thrust his hand into his robe, when he brought it out it was white and diseased. When he put it back in and drew it out, it was perfectly healthy.

Still Moses offered excuses. "Who will listen to me, Lord?" he asked. "I am not eloquent. I am slow of speech and tongue." Perhaps Moses stuttered, or maybe he was terrified of speaking in public. At any rate, when he gave this excuse, God promised that Moses' older brother, Aaron, could go with him and do the talking.

So Moses agreed at last to do what God had commanded. He confronted Pharaoh and after many trials led the people out of slavery toward the promised land of Canaan. During their forty-year journey, God appeared in fire more than once. The Biblical writer tells us that a pillar of fire led the people by night and a pillar of cloud by day so that they could travel either by day or night.

Indeed, the people came again to Sinai, the sacred mountain. This time the whole mountain seemed to be enveloped in fire. The people begged Moses to be their spokesman. "You can speak to God in the fire and not be destroyed," they said. "This great fire may burn us up. You go up on the mountain and hear what God has to say, then you can come down and tell us."

So Moses went up alone to the fiery mountain, and God gave him the Ten Commandments so that the Israelites would know how God wanted them to live.

[Retold from Exodus 1–4 and Deuteronomy 5:22–27]

Fire can be terrifying, as the people of Israel knew, but it also gives us warmth and light. Fire cleanses and purifies and is a source of power.

In the New Testament, fire is also used as a symbol of God's presence. In the book of Acts, the writer tells us that after Jesus' death and resurrection, he left the disciples, telling them to wait for the coming of God's Spirit. When the Spirit came on the Day of Pentecost, the disciples experienced God's presence in the sound of a strong wind, and they seemed to see, resting on each person's head, a tongue of fire. [Acts 2:2–3]

ROCK

For God alone my soul waits in silence;
from him comes my salvation.
He alone is my rock and my salvation,
my fortress; I shall never be shaken.

[Psalm 62:1–2]

In a landscape where there are hardly any trees, a great boulder can be seen from a long distance away. It may provide the only shade for miles, and it seems strong and immovable. Rock serves as the foundation for building and for protection from enemies. Over and over again in the Bible, rocks stand for dependability and shelter. "Trust in the Lord forever," says the prophet Isaiah [26:4], "for in the Lord God you have an everlasting rock."

Many years later, when a discouraged people were in exile in Babylon, another prophet encouraged them to remember their history and God who was the source of their life:

Listen to me, you that pursue righteousness,
　　you that seek the Lord.
Look to the rock from which you were hewn,
　　and to the quarry from which you were dug.
Look to Abraham your father
　　and to Sarah who bore you;
for he was but one when I called him,
　　but I blessed him and made him many.
For the Lord will comfort Zion;
　　he will comfort all her waste places,
and will make her wilderness like Eden,
　　her desert like the garden of the Lord;
joy and gladness will be found in her,
　　　thanksgiving and the voice of song.

[Isaiah 51:1–3]

CLOUD

The Lord went in front of them in a pillar of cloud by day to lead them along the way, and in a pillar of fire by night to give them light, so that they might travel by day and by night. Neither the pillar of cloud by day nor the pillar of fire by night left its place in front of the people. [Exodus 13:21–22]

In the wilderness wanderings God led the people of Israel. By day God's protection and guidance was seen as a pillar of cloud, by night as a pillar of fire.

Sometimes in the Bible story a cloud signifies concealment, hiding the brilliance of God's presence from the people, as in Exodus 19:16. But more often in the story of the Exodus, the cloud is intertwined with the idea of God's glory—the visible presence of God on earth—as in this passage, where the glory of God fills the special tent where the ark was kept. The ark was a sacred box that contained the Ten Commandments written on stone tablets.

Then the cloud covered the tent of meeting, and the glory of the Lord filled the tabernacle. Moses was not able to enter the tent of meeting because the cloud settled upon it, and the glory of the Lord filled the tabernacle. Whenever the cloud was taken up from the tabernacle, the Israelites would set out on each stage of their journey; but if the cloud was not taken up, then they did not set out until the day that it was taken up. For the cloud of the Lord was on the tabernacle by day, and fire was in the cloud by night, before the eyes of all the house of Israel at each stage of their journey. [Exodus 40:34–38]

Some of the Israelites worshipped the ark, as though God were present in that box, but the later prophets warned them (and us) against trying to fix God to a certain place or time. In fact, the prophet Jeremiah claimed that God intended for God's glory, God's presence, to be in the people God loved.

I made the whole house of Israel and the whole house of Judah cling to me, says the Lord, in order that they might be for me a people, a name, a praise, and a glory. But they would not listen. [Jeremiah 13:11]

DOVE

[Noah] sent out the dove from him, to see if the waters had subsided from the face of the ground. . . . [After forty-seven days] again he sent out the dove from the ark, and the dove came back to him in the evening, and there in its beak was a freshly plucked olive leaf; so Noah knew that the waters had subsided from the earth.   [Genesis 8:8–11]

And when Jesus had been baptized, just as he came up from the water, suddenly the heavens were opened to him and he saw the Spirit of God descending like a dove and alighting on him. And a voice from heaven said, "This is my Son, the Beloved, with whom I am well pleased." [Matthew 3:16–17]

Now what do these two stories have in common besides water and a dove? The story of Noah and the great flood is very familiar, but what connection

could it have with the story of Jesus' baptism in the Jordan River? In the Genesis story, God sees that people have become so evil that he decides to destroy his creation. Only Noah and his family and the animals they take with them on the ark survive the devastating flood. Now the waters are receding. Noah must determine if it is safe to land the ark and unload. The dove in the story is a messenger, bringing to Noah a sign of God's care. The leaf she carries in her beak shows that plants, too, have survived and are now flourishing. It is safe for Noah to begin his mission of starting life anew on the earth.

In the New Testament story John the Baptist is preaching by the Jordan River, calling everyone who will listen to repent of their evil ways and be baptized. He warns the people that the judgment of God is near. One day his cousin Jesus appears among the crowds and asks John to baptize him. At first John refuses, for what evil has Jesus done that he should repent and be baptized? But Jesus insists. As Matthew tells the story, when Jesus comes up out of the water, he experiences the presence of the Spirit of God like a dove coming down and lighting on his shoulder.

Up to this point the young man Jesus has been a carpenter in the town of Nazareth. Now he is about to begin the work that he was born to do. Surely he senses the difficulties ahead. Just as in the days of Noah, most people did not want God to question their way of living. They may have longed for someone especially chosen by God, a Messiah, to deliver them from the hated Roman conquerors, but most of them would not want a Messiah who cared for the poor and was a friend of prostitutes and tax collectors. So when the Gospel writer Matthew tells us that after his baptism Jesus experienced the Spirit of God "like a dove," Matthew wants us to remember the message of hope that the dove brought to Noah. Just as in that earlier story, the dove was the assurance of God's promise of new life. Now was the time for a new beginning. With this assurance of God's approval and presence, Jesus is ready to begin his ministry of teaching and healing.

EAGLE AND HEN

Then Moses went up to God; the Lord called to him from the mountain, saying, "Thus you shall say to the house of Jacob, and tell the Israelites: You have seen what I did to the Egyptians, and how I bore you on eagles' wings and brought you to myself. Now therefore, if you obey my voice and keep my covenant, you shall be my treasured possession out of all the peoples. Indeed, the whole earth is mine, but you shall be for me a priestly kingdom and a holy nation. These are the words that you shall speak to the Israelites."

[Exodus 19:3–6]

When we see an eagle in flight, we are awed by its majesty. Perhaps that is why our American ancestors, wishing to say what the tiny new nation might become, chose the eagle as our symbol of freedom and power. In Exodus, when God reminds the people of

Israel of their miraculous delivery from slavery, it is with the image of a great eagle soaring toward safety, bearing the people away on its powerful wings.

About 1,200 years later, Jesus sorrowfully uses quite a different bird to paint a picture of caring for the people of his nation.

> "Jerusalem, Jerusalem, the city that kills the prophets and stones those who are sent to it! How often I have desired to gather your children together as a hen gathers her brood under her wings, and you were not willing!" [Luke 13:34]

MAN AND WOMAN

There are two creation stories in the Bible. They sit side by side in the first and second chapters of Genesis. The first story begins with the creation of light and tells how God, on successive days, made earth and sky, water, dry land and plants, sun, moon and stars, birds and the creatures of the sea, animals of the land, and, finally, as a climax to the creation, we read these words:

> Then God said, "Let us make humankind [in Hebrew, the word is *adam*] in our image, according to our likeness; and let them have dominion over the fish of the sea, and over the birds of the air, and over the cattle, and over all the wild animals of the earth, and over every creeping thing that creeps upon the earth."

> *So God created humankind in his image,*
> *in the image of God he created them;*
> *male and female he created them.*

" . . . God saw everything that he had made, and indeed, it was very good." [Genesis 1:26–27, 31]

Scholars have argued for centuries over what the word "image" means in this passage. Does it mean that the writer thought that the first man and woman bore a bodily likeness to God? Did the writer think that God had arms and legs and human features?

Perhaps so. People many years ago did think of God as being like themselves physically. But the writer says that the image of God included male and female, so it seems that the writer was thinking of something other than people's physical bodies.

The writer of the second story of creation has God create *adam* (or humankind) first—then the world and its creatures [Genesis 2:5–7]. The center of the creation was a beautiful garden for Adam to live in and care for, but Adam was lonely in the garden, so God created a woman, as a companion for Adam to live and work with. This writer goes on to tell the tragic story of the man and woman's disobedience to the God who made them and of their expulsion from the garden God gave them.

Are we to think, then, that Adam and Eve no longer bore the "image of God" or, at best, that the image of God—humankind's likeness to God—was now badly damaged?

A Jewish scholar, W. Gunther Plaut, says that the image of God in Genesis refers to humankind's intellectual capacity, moral potential, and essential dignity.* In this sense, then,

humankind does still bear some likeness to God, although this likeness is imperfect and far from what God originally intended.

Christian writers turn to Jesus as the perfect image of God, calling him the "second Adam" or the "New Man." "He is the image of the invisible God," Paul says, "the firstborn of all creation." [Colossians 1:15]

*The Torah: A Modern Commentary. New York: Union of Hebrew Congregations, 1981.

TO EARTH COME DOWN

Images from Ordinary Life

Mother

When Israel was a child, I loved him,
    and out of Egypt I called my son.
The more I called them,
    the more they went from me;
they kept sacrificing to the Baals,
    and offering incense to idols.

Yet it was I who taught Ephraim to walk,
    I took them up in my arms;
    but they did not know that I healed them.
I led them with cords of human kindness,
    with bands of love.
I was to them like those
    who lift infants to their cheeks.
    I bent down to them and fed them.

                         [Hosea 11:1–4]

Although the English language makes us choose either masculine or feminine pronouns when we speak of persons, it is not appropriate to confine God to human gender. As the writer of Genesis 1 proclaimed, it takes both male and female to reflect the image of God. In one of the most poignant passages in the Bible, the prophet Hosea portrays God as a loving parent, calling after a willful child who will not come home. Just as a mother remembers when her child was young, God remembers all that was done for Israel in the early years. How when they stumbled, God healed them, as a loving mother picks up a crying toddler and kisses away the hurt. A mother, Hosea says, will not forget the infant she has nursed and cuddled and cared for. She will love her wayward child and grieve for him always.

Years later, when what was left of the people of Israel had been taken to Babylon as defeated captives, they complained that God had forgotten them. Another prophet answered their complaint, recalling this image of the loving mother and saying that God's love was even stronger than that of a human mother's.

> But Zion [Israel] said, "The Lord has forsaken me,
>   my Lord has forgotten me."
> Can a woman forget her nursing child,
>   or show no compassion for the child of her womb?
> Even these may forget,

yet I will not forget you.
See, I have inscribed you on the palms of my hands.

[Isaiah 49:14–16]

No, God will not forget the people. It is as though they are tattooed into the palm of God's hand.

FATHER

This is a story Jesus told to explain to his listeners what the love of God was like.

There was once a man who had two sons. The younger son grew tired of working on his father's farm, so one day he said to his father, "Father, I want you to give me now the share of your property that will someday be mine." Reluctantly, his father divided his property and gave his younger son his share.

The son was delighted. At last, he thought, I'm free. I can go wherever I want and do whatever I choose. He took all the money his father had given him and went off to a distant country. There he did all the things he had never dared to do when he was home. He had plenty of friends, men and women who loved helping him spend his fortune. He was having the time of his life, but before too long he had spent all of his inheritance. The friends who had clung to him when he was rich disappeared. If he looked them up to ask for help, they pretended not to know him. No one was willing to give him anything.

He knew he had to find work, but the only job he was able to find was as a pig keeper. He was so hungry that sometimes he tried to eat the slops thrown out for the pigs.

One day as he watched the pigs, he thought of his home. His father's lowliest slaves always had plenty to eat, and he was starving. "I'll go home," he decided. "I'll say to my father, 'Father, I've sinned against heaven and against you. I'm not worthy to be called your son, I know. Just make me one of your hired servants.'" And so he started his long journey home.

Meanwhile, his heartbroken father was worrying about his son. Where could he be? Was he all right? Would he ever come home again? He would often look down the road, the same road his son had taken, and long to see him coming back again.

Then one day, his eyes straining, he saw the form of a man, far down the road. Could that ragged beggar be his missing boy? It was, it was, he was sure it was! The old man gathered up his robes and began to run. He ran all the way to the startled boy, threw his arms around him, and kissed him.

"Father—" His son began the speech he had rehearsed over and over as he walked. "I have sinned against heaven and against you. I'm not worthy to be called your son . . ."

But his father wasn't even listening. He called to his slaves, "Hurry, bring out the best robe and put it on him, bring sandals for his feet, and a ring for his finger. Go out and get the calf we have fattened and kill it. We must eat and celebrate, for

my son who was dead is alive again, the one who was lost is found!"

So the slaves obeyed, a great feast was prepared, and the celebration began.

Now the elder son was off working in a distant field, but as he came home, the music from the party was so loud that he heard it before he reached the house. He called out to a slave to ask what was going on inside.

"Your brother has come home," the slave replied, "and your father has killed the fatted calf and is throwing a great party for him."

When he heard this, the older brother was furious and refused to go into the house. His father came out and pleaded with him to come in and join the party. "Why should I come in?" he answered angrily. "I've been working like a slave for you all these years. I've done everything you've asked me to without complaint, and you never even gave me a baby goat to celebrate with my friends. But when this son of yours who went off and ate up all your inheritance with prostitutes, when *he* comes home, you kill the fatted calf!"

Then the father put his arm around his angry son and said sadly, "Son, you have always been with me. Everything I have is yours. But don't you see? We have to celebrate and rejoice. Your brother who was dead is alive again—your brother who was lost is found." [Retold from Luke 15:11–32]

HOUSEWIFE

"Or what woman having ten silver coins, if she loses one of them, does not light a lamp, sweep the house, and search carefully until she finds it? When she has found it, she calls together her friends and neighbors, saying, 'Rejoice with me, for I have found the coin that I had lost.' Just so, I tell you, there is joy in the presence of the angels of God over one sinner who repents." [Luke 15:8–10]

Jesus had a keen eye for many of the small but still important happenings of everyday life. He himself had been raised in a modest home, as had most of his friends. One silver coin would be the equivalent of about a day's wages for a laborer in those days. So when Jesus needed to give an example of the careful persistence of God in searching after people who have gone astray, he told a story of a housewife who put everything aside to look for a lost coin. This single coin was of great value to her, even though she had nine others, and she did

not give up sweeping every dark corner until she found it. When she did find it at last, she called in all her friends and neighbors to share her joy. This, said Jesus, is the kind of joy that goes on in heaven when a single person turns back and opens his or her life to the love of God.

Visitor

One hot day Abraham was sitting in front of his tent under the shade of the terebinth trees when he saw three weary travelers coming down the road.

In the manner of a gracious Middle Eastern host, Abraham invited the travelers to rest in the shade. After he had brought water to wash their dusty feet, he hurried into the tent to ask his wife, Sarah, to bake some bread and sent a servant to kill and prepare a calf so that his visitors would have food to eat to refresh them for their journey.

As he stood by while his visitors ate their meal, making sure that his visitors lacked nothing, one of the men said to Abraham, "Where is your wife, Sarah?"

"Why," said Abraham, surprised that the stranger would know his wife's name, "she is in the tent just yonder."

"Before long," the visitor continued, "your wife will have a son."

Now Sarah was eavesdropping just inside the tent and when she heard the visitor say that she would have a child, she almost laughed out loud. "At my age?" she said to herself. "It's impossible. I'm far too old to have a baby."

It was almost as if the visitor could read her thoughts, for he said to Abraham, "Why is Sarah laughing? Is anything impossible for God? When the time comes, I will return, and Sarah will indeed have a child."

Then Sarah was frightened. Who was this stranger? "I didn't laugh," she said.

"Yes, you did," the man said. But he and his companions had other business that day. "We have heard of the cities of Sodom and Gomorrah, how wicked they are. I must go down there and see for myself." The two companions went ahead to Sodom, but by now Abraham realized that the visitor who stayed behind was the Lord himself.

"Are you planning to destroy the city?" he asked the Lord. "Will you just sweep away the good people with the bad, the righteous along with the wicked? How could you do that? Shouldn't the Judge of all the earth do what is just? Suppose there are fifty good people in the city, would you just destroy it and not forgive it for the sake of those fifty righteous who live there?"

"If I find fifty righteous people there, I will forgive the whole place for their sake."

Now Abraham's nephew Lot and his family lived in that city, and so he dared to bargain with the Lord. "Suppose there are only forty-five righteous people in Sodom," he said. "Would you destroy the city for lack of five good people?"

"No," said the Lord. "I would not destroy it if I found forty-five righteous there."

"Suppose there are only forty?"

"For the sake of forty I would not destroy it."

Then Abraham said, "Please don't be angry if I say it, but suppose thirty are there."

"I will not do it if I find thirty."

Abraham knew he was treading on dangerous ground but he couldn't count thirty people in Sodom whom he thought God would call righteous, so he continued his bargaining. "Let me just take it upon myself to suggest that perhaps only twenty will be found there. What then?"

"For the sake of twenty, I would not destroy the city," the Lord answered patiently.

"Oh, don't be angry if I speak just once more to the Lord. Suppose ten are found there."

The Lord replied, "For the sake of ten, I will not destroy Sodom." And with that the Lord went on his way.

When the Lord came to Sodom, we are told, not even ten righteous people could be found. So both cities were destroyed, although Lot, his wife, and his two daughters were given a chance to escape first.

"Flee for your lives," the visitors commanded them, "but do not stop on the Plain or look back until you are safely in the hills."

But, we are told, Lot's wife looked back as they crossed the

Plain and she was turned into a pillar of salt, while Lot and his daughters reached the hills and were saved.

Sometime later a son was born to Abraham and Sarah, and Sarah named him Isaac, which means laughter, for as she said, "God has brought laughter for me, and everyone who hears about my son will laugh with me."

[Retold from Genesis 18, 19, and 21]

Note: In the Genesis account of this story, the visitors are sometimes three, sometimes two, sometimes one. Sometimes they are called "the men" and at other times "angel," though the single visitor with whom Abraham bargains is identified as "the Lord." The word angel means "messenger" and is not always meant to be a supernatural figure, but certainly the men in this account seem to be heavenly beings if not representations of God. In the New Testament, as in the visit of Gabriel to Mary to tell of the birth of Jesus, angels seem more often to be heavenly beings and not simply human beings with a heavenly message, though perhaps people cannot always tell the difference. The writer of the book of Hebrews, in admonishing the early Christians to be hospitable, says (and surely he is remembering the story of Abraham and the Visitors when he does so): "Do not neglect to show hospitality to strangers, for by doing that some have entertained angels without knowing it." [Hebrews 13:2]

HOST

Suppose you decide to give a great banquet, a marvelous party, for all your friends. You send out the invitations and make all the preparations for the feast, but on the appointed evening no one shows up. Imagine how you'd feel. You begin calling everyone up on the phone. Where are you? Why aren't you here? And all you get from your friends are excuses. Nobody you invited is going to come to your party. What will you do? In Luke, Jesus tells just such a story.

There was once a man who decided to give a great banquet. There would be wonderful food, music, and dancing—a great celebration for all his friends. He sent out many invitations, and everyone said they would come. He was delighted. He loved parties and he wanted this particular dinner to be the best party he had ever given.

"Don't worry about the expense," he told the cook. "Buy the best food and drink you can find and make sure there is plenty of everything. I want this to be a meal my friends will long remember."

It took days to prepare for such a feast, but they were days the man enjoyed. He was a generous and gracious host, and he loved to think of what a good time he and his friends would have together.

Finally the long-awaited evening arrived. He sent his servant out to tell his guests that everything was ready for the feast.

But to the servant's surprise, all the people who had responded enthusiastically to the invitation now began to make excuses. One of them said to the servant: "Of course, I'd love to come to your master's party, but it just so happens that I have bought a piece of land, and I'm just on the way out to look at it. Please give my regrets."

A second invited guest said, "You've caught me at a bad time. I really had expected to come to the party, but I've just bought five yoke of oxen and I can't wait to try them out. Do accept my regrets."

A third guest said: "I'm sure the host will understand. I've just gotten married, and you know the law says that a new husband should not be compelled to go to war or be charged with business so that he can stay home for a year and be with his new wife. So as you see, I can't possibly come."

And so it went, down the entire guest list. Every single one of the invited guests gave the servant some excuse and sent his regrets to the host who was expecting him.

When the servant returned and told the host that none of the invited guests was coming to his banquet, the host was angry. After all, he had gone to enormous trouble and expense

for this great feast. Why had all his friends refused to come? And most of them with the flimsiest of excuses.

He said to his servant: "Go out then, and find the poor, the crippled, the blind, the lame. Bring them in to eat my dinner."

The servant went out and found as many crippled, blind, and lame beggars as he could and invited them to the great table, but there was still room for more people.

So the host ordered the servant to find more guests. "Go out into the roads and lanes, search out the highways and the hedges, find anyone and everyone you can and bring them in. I want my house to be filled, for none of my friends that I invited will taste my banquet." [Retold from Luke 14:16–24]

God is such a host, Jesus seems to be saying. God wants everyone to enjoy the bounties of his love. God is a gracious host, not because we deserve this graciousness, but because it is God's nature to be gracious. But we can choose. We can refuse to come to God's party. Like the rude and foolish friends in Jesus' story, we can stay away and miss out on the celebration.

WRESTLER

Jacob was on his way home. He should have been happy. He had been away twenty years in the land of Haran. He had left home with nothing; he was returning with wives and children and servants, with flocks of sheep and goats and herds of cows and donkeys and camels.

But Jacob was afraid. For between him and home his brother, Esau, was waiting. Jacob and Esau were the twin sons of Isaac and his wife Rebekah. Esau was born first, all hairy and red, and was named Esau, which means "hairy." The younger twin was born almost immediately, clutching his older brother's heel. So he was named "heel holder" or "the one who trips up." Jacob's name was a fitting one, because twice he had tripped up his older brother. First, he'd tricked Esau into selling his birthright, which meant that on Isaac's death, Jacob would be head of the family and get most of the property. Then, at his mother's insistence and with her conniving, Jacob had disguised himself and received from their father the blessing that should have gone to his older brother as well.

Esau was furious when this happened and swore that when-their father died, he would kill Jacob. But Rebekah, determined to protect her favorite, sent Jacob to live with her brother's family in the land of Haran. In Haran Jacob got some of his own medicine. His uncle, Laban, was a sly fellow himself. But Jacob got the best of him in the end, and now, to escape his wily uncle, he was taking his family and flocks home to Canaan.

Perhaps if he sent a gift ahead to Esau, Esau would forgive him for the wrong he had done him.

The messengers Jacob sent came back. "Esau is on the way to meet you," they said, "and he has with him a company of four hundred men."

What should Jacob do? First he divided his huge caravan in half, thinking that if Esau met one half, at least the other half would escape. Then he prayed. "Oh God of my father Abraham and my father Isaac," he said, "you told me to come home to my country. I'm not worthy of the love and faithful-ness you have shown me, because when I crossed the Jordan River before I had only the staff I carried in my hand. Now I have two great companies. I ask you, please, deliver me from Esau. I'm afraid of him. He may come kill us all, the mothers with the children. If he kills us, how can your promise be ful-filled? Remember you said to me that you would do me good and give me descendants that would be as the sand of the sea—so many that they could not be counted?"

The next morning Jacob chose from all his possessions a

great gift for Esau—two hundred female goats and twenty male goats, two hundred ewes and twenty rams, thirty milk camels and their colts, forty cows and ten bulls, twenty female donkeys and ten male donkeys. He sent these ahead with his servants, telling them to space out the droves of animals. "When Esau my brother meets you and asks 'Whose are these?' and 'Where are you going?' you are to tell him that they belong 'to your servant Jacob and he is behind us.'"

That same night he sent his two wives and their two maids, and his eleven children, across at the ford of the Jabbock River. Jacob stayed alone on the other side. He could not sleep. He was too anxious for what the next day might bring.

Then he realized that he was not alone. There seemed to be someone with him, a man, who grasped him and threw him to the ground. Jacob fought back. The man was strong, but Jacob was determined. Whoever or whatever it was would not conquer him. They wrestled on and on, neither of them defeating the other, for although Jacob grew tired, he struggled back each time. As day was breaking, the stranger reached out and touched Jacob's thigh, putting Jacob's hip out of joint; but even lamed, Jacob would not let go.

"Let me go," the wrestler said. "It is nearly dawn."

"No," said Jacob, who by now realized that this was no ordinary mortal he was struggling with, "no, I won't let you go until you bless me."

"What is your name?"

"Jacob."

"Your name is not going to be Jacob any longer. From now on your name will be Israel, for you have struggled both with divine and human beings and you have prevailed."

Then Jacob said, "Tell me who you are. What is your name?"

But the wrestler answered, "Why do you ask me what my name is?" And he blessed Jacob and disappeared.

Jacob named the place where the wrestling match took place "Peniel," which means "the face of God," for he said, "I have seen God face to face, and yet my life has been preserved."

Then he left Peniel to face his brother Esau, but from that time on he limped because of the wound he had received there.   [Retold from Genesis 32:3–32]

BREAD

"For their hunger you gave them bread from heaven, and for their thirst you brought water for them out of the rock, and you told them to go in to possess the land that you swore to give them." [Nehemiah 9:15]

In this prayer, the priest Ezra recalls all that God has done for the Israelites from the call of Abraham to the present. The people listening to this prayer are a small remnant of the nation that was defeated by the Babylonians in 586 B.C. At that time the Babylonians destroyed Jerusalem and took the people away as captives. Now after years of exile in Babylon, the new world power, the Persians, who defeated the Babylonians, have given permission for those Jews (as they will be called from now on) to return to their homeland. It's a discouraging sight that greets the Jews in 538 B.C. Their beautiful city lies in ruins, the walls are rubble, the great temple of Solomon with all its treasures, which they had thought would last forever, is gone.

But Ezra and Nehemiah, two of the leaders of the returnees, will not let the people give up. They begin to rebuild the wall so as to have some protection from their hostile neighbors, and eventually they build another temple as well. Not so grand a building as Solomon with all his wealth had erected, but a sign of hope and new life for the community.

Ezra calls the people together, not long after the wall has been completed. He wants to remind them that the most important thing to be repaired is neither walls nor buildings, but their relationship to God. He calls upon them to confess to God that they have broken the law Moses gave them. He reminds them of all God has done through their ancestors, and especially in the Exodus from Egypt and the wanderings in the wilderness, and urges them to renew their covenant—their promise—to God to be the people of God, obeying God's law. [Nehemiah 7, 8, 9]

One sign that all Israel's leaders saw as evidence of God's love and care was the manna in the wilderness. Not long after the Israelites escaped from Egypt, they found themselves in the desert. There was nothing to eat there, and they began to complain to Moses. They seemed to have completely forgotten all God had done to free them. "If only we had died by the hand of the Lord in the land of Egypt," they said, "when we sat by the fleshpots and ate our fill of bread; for you have brought us out into this wilderness to kill this whole assembly with hunger."

In answer to their complaints, God told Moses, "I am going

to rain bread from heaven for you. . . ." This "bread" was a kind of flaky substance that the Israelites called manna (which means "What is it?" since the Israelites had never seen the like before). [Exodus 16:1—7] At first the people were very grateful for the manna, but by and by they got bored eating the same old thing every day and began complaining again. [Numbers 11:6]

Still, throughout the Hebrew Bible and the Christian New Testament, the bread from heaven is an image of God's continuous loving care.

In Psalm 78, the writer reminds the people of God's goodness throughout their history despite their doubts and disobedience.

> *Yet he commanded the skies above,*
>   *and opened the doors of heaven;*
> *He rained down on them manna to eat,*
>   *and gave them the grain of heaven.*
> *Mortals ate of the bread of angels;*
>   *he sent them food in abundance.*
>
> [Psalm 78:23–24]

In the 55th chapter of Isaiah, the prophet who sought to encourage the Jews while they were still in exile in Babylon wrote this invitation from God:

> *"Ho, everyone who thirsts,*
>   *come to the waters;*

and you that have no money,
      come, buy and eat!
Come, buy wine and milk
      without money and without price.
Why do you spend your money
      for that which is not bread,
and your labor for that
      which does not satisfy?
Listen carefully to me, and eat
      what is good,
      and delight yourselves in rich food."

[Isaiah 55:1–2]

When, many years later, Jesus speaks of his own mission from God, he calls to mind both this invitation to God's bounty and the image of God's loving kindness—the bread of heaven.

"I am the bread of life," he said. "Your ancestors ate the manna in the wilderness, and they died. This is the bread that comes down from heaven, so that one may eat of it and not die. I am the living bread that came down from heaven. Whoever eats of this bread will live forever; and the bread that I will give for the life of the world is my flesh." [John 6:48–51] Needless to say, these words seemed very puzzling, if not blasphemous, to those who heard them.

WITH A MIGHTY HAND

Images of Watchfulness and Creation

LANDOWNER

Jesus told this story to explain that the justice of God is different from human ideas of justice.

The kingdom of heaven, Jesus told his followers, is like an owner of great lands who went out to the market-place at sunrise to hire laborers to work in his vine-yard. The owner and the workers first agreed on what he would pay them for their day's work. It would be one denarius, a usual day's wage. Then he sent them into his vineyard to pick the ripe grapes.

The vineyards were vast, and the grapes had to be picked before the rains came and ruined them, so at about nine o'clock, the landowner went back to the marketplace, where he found other men looking for work. He hired them, saying: "Go work in my vineyard and I'll pay you whatever is right."

Again at noon, and then again at three o'clock he went back

to the marketplace, found more laborers looking for work, and sent them into his vineyards as well.

At five o'clock in the afternoon, an hour before the workday ended, he went once more to the marketplace and saw other men standing about. "Why aren't you working?" the land-owner asked them. "Why have you stood about idle all day?"

"We want to work," the men answered, "but no one will hire us."

"Go work in my vineyard," the owner said.

When six o'clock came, the owner told the steward to assemble the workers so they could be paid, beginning with those hired last and going on to those hired at dawn.

When the ones who had been hired at five o'clock presented themselves to the owner, he paid each one of them a denarius. He also paid the workers who had come at three and at noon and at nine o'clock a denarius each. The ones who had been working since dawn thought they would receive more—after all, they had put in a full day's work; but when their time came to be paid, they received a denarius as well.

The early workers began to complain against the landowner. "The men who came last have worked only one hour, and the owner has paid them the same thing he has paid us who worked all day through the heat," they said.

The owner heard their grumbling and called them over. "Didn't we agree that I would pay you one denarius for the day's work?" he asked.

"Yes, but . . ."

"Take what you have earned and go home," the owner said. "It was my choice what I would pay these last, and I have chosen to give them the same wages that I have paid you. Am I not allowed to do what I wish with what is mine? Why are you envious because I have chosen to be generous?"

[Retold from Matthew 20:1–15]

The earth is the Lord's and all that is in it,
the world, and those who live in it;
for he has founded it on the seas,
and established it on the rivers.

[Psalm 24:1–2]

GARDENER

Jesus said:

> "I am the real vine, and my Father is the gardener. Every barren branch of mine he cuts away; and every fruiting branch he cleans, to make it more fruitful still." [John 15:1–2 New English Bible]

Have you ever pruned a grapevine? It doesn't make the gardener happy to cut off and cart away a lot of spindly but obviously healthy shoots, but if the job is not done, the vitality of the vine will be sapped. A lot of green shoots will produce many leaves but very little fruit, while a few strong branches, properly pruned, can produce many good grapes. Someone who didn't understand what the gardener was doing might argue that the grapevine was being treated badly, even cruelly. But the gardener knows what is best and acts accordingly.

The John 15 passage pictures God as a gardener who not only nourishes his vines but is willing to prune them so that an abundance of grapes will result. What might seem harsh treatment of the vine is really for the sake of the vine, so that it may produce the richest harvest possible.

The Apostle Paul took this image a step further. The gardener (or husbandman, as he is also called) often grafts a shoot from another stock onto a vine or a tree to produce a new or stronger variety of fruit. He says the Gentiles (those outside the people of Israel) were like a wild olive shoot that God chose to graft onto the cultivated tree that was the Jews—the original people of the Covenant.* [Romans 11:17–24]

*The word "covenant" appears throughout the Bible. It means "agreement" or "bond" and it was used originally to describe the special relationship that God had with certain individuals, such as Noah and Abraham. In later years it defined the relationship between God and the Israelites, continuing with the Jewish nation that descended from the children of Israel. The word "testament" means "covenant," and the Christian "New Testament" or "New Covenant" tells of Jesus, who Christians believe gave a new covenant meant not only for the children of Israel but for all who would accept God's love.

POTTER

The word that came to Jeremiah from the Lord: "Come, go down to the potter's house, and there I will let you hear my words." So I went down to the potter's house, and there he was working at his wheel. The vessel he was making of clay was spoiled in the potter's hand, and he reworked it into another vessel, as seemed good to him.

Then the word of the Lord came to me: Can I not do with you, O house of Israel, just as this potter has done? says the Lord. Just like the clay in the potter's hand, so are you in my hand, O house of Israel. At one moment I may declare concerning a nation or a kingdom, that I will pluck up and break down and destroy it, but if that nation, concerning which I have spoken, turns from its evil, I will change my mind about the disaster that I intended to bring on it . . . but if it does evil in my sight, not listening to my voice, then I will change my mind about the good that I had

intended to do to it. Now, therefore, say to the people of Judah and the inhabitants of Jerusalem: Thus says the Lord: Look, I am a potter shaping evil against you and devising a plan against you. Turn now, all of you from your evil way, and amend your ways and your doings." [Jeremiah 18:1–11]

One of the delightful features of clay is the possibility of its being shaped and reshaped. The potter can take a bit of wet clay and fashion it into a bowl, but if the bowl doesn't please him, he can ball it up and start all over again. The potter is in charge. The clay does not tell the potter what to do; it is the potter who makes the choice.

In using this image of the potter and the clay, Jeremiah was trying to wake up the people to the impending destruction of their nation. The people had long ago forgotten the promises they had made at Mount Sinai to be God's people and obey God's law. The Israelites had divided into two kingdoms about 930 B.C., and the Northern Kingdom, which continued to be called Israel, was destroyed by the Assyrians about 722 B.C. The tiny Southern Kingdom, known as Judah, struggled on against mighty foes. The city of Jerusalem was miraculously saved when the Assyrian army was struck down by a mysterious plague just as they were about to overrun the city.

Even a hundred years later the memory of this miraculous deliverance made the people of Judah arrogant. Why should they worry that the Babylonians were headed for their city, intent on defeating them? God was present in the temple of Jerusalem. Therefore they had nothing to fear. God would never allow Jerusalem to be destroyed. But the prophet Jeremiah said this was a false hope. In their pride and disobedience the people had become like a spoiled vessel in the hand of the potter. But the potter was not helpless. The potter would roll the spoiled piece into a formless ball of clay, where it could be reshaped into a worthy and useful creation.

SHEPHERD

The shepherd is one of the most frequently used images for God in the Bible. The Jews came from a nomadic people who were dependent on their flocks of sheep for food and clothing. The work of the shepherd was vital. Jacob took care of his father-in-law's sheep before he had flocks of his own, and when he blessed his son Joseph before his death, he spoke of "the God who has been my shepherd all my life to this day." [Genesis 48:15] Moses was herding his father-in-law's sheep when God spoke to him from the burning bush.

Even after the Israelites settled in Canaan, the work of sheep herding continued. As a boy David, who became Israel's greatest king, was a shepherd. He is credited with the familiar shepherd psalm or hymn, as well as many of the other psalms.

The Lord is my shepherd, I shall not want.
He makes me lie down in green pastures;
He leads me beside still waters;
he restores my soul.

He leads me in right paths
for his name's sake.

Even though I walk through the darkest valley,
I fear no evil;
for you are with me;
your rod and your staff—
they comfort me.

You prepare a table before me
in the presence of my enemies;
you anoint my head with oil;
my cup overflows.
Surely goodness and mercy shall follow me
all the days of my life,
and I shall dwell in the house of the Lord
my whole life long.   [Psalm 23]

The picture of the strong, fearless shepherd tenderly caring for his sheep was a very powerful and comforting image. When the prophet Ezekiel wanted to show how wicked the rulers of Israel had been, he painted them as false shepherds who cared for themselves rather than for the sheep entrusted to them.

"Thus says the Lord God: Ah, you shepherds of Israel who have been feeding yourselves! Should not shep-

herds feed the sheep? You eat the fat, you clothe yourselves with the wool, you slaughter the fatlings; but
you do not feed the sheep. You have not strengthened
the weak, you have not healed the sick, you have not
bound up the injured, you have not brought back the
strayed, you have not sought the lost, but with force
and harshness you have ruled them. So they were scattered, because there was no shepherd; and scattered,
they became food for all the wild animals.

[Ezekiel 34:2–5]

In contrast, the prophet of the exile promises that God will
care for the scattered and hurting flock.

He will feed his flock like a shepherd;
he will gather the lambs in his arms,
and carry them in his bosom,
and gently lead the mother sheep.

[Isaiah 40:11]

Jesus also spoke of God as the good shepherd who leaves
ninety-nine sheep in the fold and goes out to search for the one
that is lost; and when he finds it, he puts it on his shoulders and
carries it home rejoicing. [Luke 15:1–7] In explaining to his disciples his own mission, Jesus again used the image of the shepherd.

"I am the good shepherd. The good shepherd lays
down his life for the sheep. The hired hand, who is not

the shepherd and does not own the sheep, sees the wolf coming and leaves the sheep and runs away— and the wolf snatches them and scatters them. The hired hand runs away because a hired hand does not care for the sheep. I am the good shepherd. I know my own and my own know me, just as the Father knows me and I know the Father. And I lay down my life for the sheep. I have other sheep that do not belong to this fold. I must bring them also, and they will listen to my voice. So there will be one flock, one shepherd."

[John 10:11–16]

JUDGE

Sometimes we get so solemn about the Bible that we miss the humor in it. Jesus told this story about a judge to remind his disciples that they should never grow tired of coming to God with their prayers.

In a certain city there lived a judge. Now this judge had no respect for either God or man. He did whatever he pleased with little concern for true justice. It happened that in that same city there lived a poor widow woman who had been cheated by an unscrupulous man, so she went to the judge's court to ask the judge for help. The judge couldn't be bothered with the concerns of this poor woman. He refused even to see her.

The woman, however, was persistent. She came to the court every day asking that the judge see her and settle her complaint. Every time the judge left his house, there she was, demanding to be heard. He couldn't go anywhere without the widow trailing him about, calling out to him for justice.

At first the judge tried to ignore her. It just made the woman noisier. Then he sent her away, telling her that he would not judge on her complaint. But the widow simply would not be discouraged. She plagued him day and night, demanding to be heard.

At last the unjust judge said to himself: "I may not have any fear of God or respect for any person, but this woman is going to run me crazy. I am going to grant her justice just to keep her from wearing me out with her nonstop demands."

"Listen to what the unjust judge says," Jesus said. "If he will grant justice, won't God listen to his children who cry to him day and night? I promise you God will quickly grant them justice." [Retold from Luke 18:1–8]

There are many instances in the Bible where God is spoken of as judge. When Abraham was pleading that God not destroy the wicked cities of Sodom and Gomorrah for the sake of the few good people who lived in them, he argued: "Shall not the Judge of all the earth do what is just?" [Genesis 18:25]

Abraham's argument is echoed throughout the Bible. God, who created the world, is also the judge of the world. But God is not like a human judge; God judges with righteousness and equity and with particular mercy for the poor and the oppressed.

In Matthew 25, Jesus gives a powerful picture of judgment:

> Then the king will say to those at his right hand, "Come, you that are blessed by my Father, inherit the kingdom prepared for you from the foundation of the

world; for I was hungry and you gave me food, I was thirsty and you gave me something to drink, I was a stranger and you welcomed me, I was naked and you gave me clothing, I was sick and you took care of me, I was in prison and you visited me."

The righteous are amazed. "Lord," they ask, "when did we see you in need and do all these things for you?" And the king answers: "Truly I tell you, just as you did it to one of the least of these who are members of my family, you did it to me." In contrast the king commands those at his left hand to depart into eternal punishment, for they have failed to show mercy to the least of God's children and therefore they have failed the king himself. In this story Jesus seems to be saying that the image of the Son of God is to be found not only in the judge of all the earth but in those who are hungry and thirsty, strangers in need of welcome, the naked in need of clothing, the sick and those in prison. [Matthew 25:34–46]

In Psalm 82, the writer pictures God holding judgment and saying in the midst of a divine assembly:

> *"How long will you judge unjustly*
> *and show partiality to the wicked?*
> *Give justice to the weak and the orphan;*
> *maintain the right of the lowly and the destitute.*

Rescue the weak and the needy;
deliver them from the hand of the wicked."

[Psalm 82:2–4]

The writers of the New Testament took the judgment of God seriously. They echoed the theme of the Hebrew prophets, who spoke of "the day of the Lord," a time when God would judge all nations and especially the people chosen to share God's justice and mercy with the world.

Although most of us think God should make the wicked pay for all their evildoing, we are uncomfortable with the idea of God as judge. Perhaps we are not so eager for God to judge us. It calls to mind the medieval paintings of God or Christ sending people off to the fires and tortures of hell, which the artists seemed to enjoy painting in gory detail. But as one theologian has said: "The Lord's judgment means putting things right, not destroying them."* If we believed this, then we would understand the prayer of the Psalmist: "Judge me, O Lord, according to my righteousness" [Psalm 7:8], because we would want God to set us right. And we don't need to be afraid, for as Jesus said to Nicodemus: "God did not send the Son into the world to condemn the world, but in order that the world might be saved [accepted by God] through him." [John 3:17]

*Pavel Filipi, "The Servant of the Lord," in *Best Sermons,* James W. Cox, editor. New York: HarperCollins, 1991, p. 198.

KING

In the year that King Uzziah died, I saw the Lord sitting on a throne, high and lofty; and the hem of his robe filled the temple. Seraphs were in attendance above him; each had six wings: with two they covered their faces, and with two they covered their feet, and with two they flew. And one called to another and said:

> *"Holy, holy, holy is the Lord of hosts;*
> *the whole earth is full of his glory."*

The pivots on the thresholds shook at the voices of those who called, and the house filled with smoke. And I said: "Woe is me! I am lost, for I am a man of unclean lips, and I live among a people of unclean lips; yet my eyes have seen the King, the Lord of hosts!"

[Isaiah 6:1–5]

Uzziah had been king of the nation of Judah for about thirty-five years. His son Jotham barely survived him, and the new king, his grandson Ahaz, was a weakling. It was a time of great crisis for Judah. The Assyrian empire was growing more and more powerful. The kingdoms of Israel and Damascus were attacking his tiny nation, and King Ahaz made an alliance with the emperor of Assyria in the vain hope that he could save his throne.

Isaiah, a young nobleman, would have been fully aware of what was happening. He tells us that during this time he went to the temple and there he had a vision, not of the beloved king who had died, but of God the Everlasting King. God called the shepherd Moses from a burning bush on the side of a mountain [Exodus 3:4], but five hundred years later God called the aristocratic Isaiah through an overwhelming vision in the temple that King Solomon had built for the nation.

The mission God gave Moses was to save the Israelites from captivity and to lead them to the land God promised to Abraham. Isaiah's mission was to tell the people of Judah that their cities would be laid waste and their people taken captive, but that out of this devastation God would preserve a tiny remnant of the people who not only would return to Judah but who would be God's witness to the whole world.

The word that Isaiah son of Amoz saw concerning Judah and Jerusalem.

In days to come
> *the mountain of the Lord's house*
shall be established as the highest of the mountains,
> *and shall be raised above the hills;*
all the nations shall stream to it.
> *Many peoples shall come and say,*
"Come, let us go up to the mountain of the Lord,
> *to the house of the God of Jacob;*
that he may teach us his ways
> *and that we may walk in his paths."*
For out of Zion shall go forth instruction,
> *and the word of the Lord from Jerusalem.*
He shall judge between the nations,
> *and shall arbitrate for many peoples;*
they shall beat their swords into plowshares,
> *and their spears into pruning hooks;*
nation shall not lift up sword against nation,
> *neither shall they learn war any more.*

[Isaiah 2:1–4]

In a world torn apart by warring kings, Isaiah spoke of a time when God would rule over a kingdom of universal justice and peace. It is a vision that still gives us hope some 2,700 years later.

ARCHITECT

Then I saw a new heaven and a new earth; for the first heaven and the first earth had passed away, and the sea was no more. And I saw the holy city, the new Jerusalem, coming down out of heaven from God, prepared as a bride adorned for her husband. And I heard a loud voice from the throne saying,

> "See, the home of God is among mortals.
> He will dwell with them as their God;
> they will be his peoples,
> and God himself will be with them;
> he will wipe every tear from their eyes.
> Death will be no more;
> mourning and crying and pain will be no more,
> for the first things have passed away."

And the one who was seated on the throne said, "See, I am making all things new." [Revelation 21:1–5]

A child in a nursery school piles blocks upon blocks, pretending to build a house. A youngster on the beach mounds wet sand into the walls and turrets of a castle. Long before we learn the word "architect," we become builders, mirroring, however faintly, the image of the Maker.

In the final book of the New Testament John sees God not only as king and creator, but as the architect of a totally new creation—a heavenly Jerusalem—infinitely more glorious than any human mind could imagine or hands construct. It is the place that the patriarchs and prophets longed for. The writer of the book of Hebrews, speaking of the faith of Abraham, says that Abraham had been willing to leave his homeland and live in tents: "For he looked forward to the city that has foundations, whose architect and builder is God." [Hebrews 11:10]

And yet it is the faith of the Bible that the design of God for creation is something to be realized not simply after death or beyond history, but here and now, in the patterns of our own lives and in the history of our own times.

The Apostle Paul, writing to Gentile believers in the city of Ephesus, said: "So then you are no longer strangers and aliens, but you are citizens with the saints and also members of the household of God, built upon the foundation of the apostles and prophets, with Christ Jesus himself as the cornerstone." [Ephesians 2:19–20]

When Jesus, who was a carpenter in Nazareth, sought to explain to his friends and neighbors the call he had from God, he read this passage from the scroll of Isaiah:

"The spirit of the Lord God is upon me,
because he has anointed me
to bring good news to the poor.
He has sent me to proclaim release to the captives
and recovery of sight to the blind,
to let the oppressed go free,
to proclaim the year of the Lord's favor."

[Luke 4:18–19]

As Jesus knew, God intends us, created as we are in God's image, to do the work of God in this world. We, too, are invited to become apprentices to the Divine Architect as we help build upon God's design for the world—working as God intends for the establishment of justice, compassion, and peace.

BIBLICAL REFERENCES

INDEX

father, 11, 55-58, 85, 94, 96
fire, 31-35, 38, 40

gardener, 85-86
Genesis, Book of, 22, 28, 41, 42, 46-47, 53, 74, 90, 96
God,
    face of, 74
    glory of, 16, 17, 38, 40
    kingdom of, 23-25, 26
    name of, 33-34
    presence of, 16, 35, 38, 40
    as spirit, 12, 20, 26
    Spirit of, 22, 28, 35, 41, 43, 107
    throne of, 22, 100
Gomorrah, 62, 96
Gospels, 13
    see also John, Gospel of; Luke, Gospel of; Matthew, Gospel of

Hebrews, 30-31
    see also Israelites
Hebrews, Book of, 65, 106
hen, 45
Hosea, 52, 53
host, 66-69
housewife, 59-60
humankind, 46, 47-48
    see also man; woman

"I am," 33
idol, idolatry, 11, 52
Isaac, 31, 33, 65, 70, 71
Isaiah, Book of, 36-37, 53-54, 78-79, 92, 100-103, 106-7
Israelites, 18, 29-35, 38-40, 44-45, 52-54, 75-78, 86, 87-89, 90, 91, 101
    see also Hebrews

Jacob, 29, 31, 33, 44, 70-74, 90
    named Israel, 74
    well of, 19
Jeremiah, 23, 89
Jeremiah, Book of, 21, 40, 87-88
Jerusalem, 16, 20, 45, 88-89
Jerusalem, new, 105, 106
Jesus, 13, 17, 18-21, 23-27, 41-42, 43, 45, 49, 65, 79, 85, 86, 96, 99, 106-7
    as shepherd, 92-94
    as Son of God, 41, 98, 99
    as storyteller, 55-58, 59-60, 66-69, 82-84, 95-98
Jews, 75
    see also Israelites
John, Gospel of, 21, 23-27, 79, 85-86, 92, 94, 99, 106
John the Baptist, 43
Joseph (son of Jacob), 29, 30, 31, 90
Joseph of Arimathea, 27
Judah, 88, 89, 101
Judaism, 11, 12-13, 47-48
judge, 62, 95-99

king, 12, 96, 97, 98, 100-103, 106
Koshkin, Alexander, 12

Lamb, 22
landowner, 82-84
light, 12, 16-17, 46
Lot, 62, 64-65
Lot's wife, 64-65
Luke, Gospel of, 45, 58, 59, 66, 69, 92, 96, 107

man, 28, 47, 49, 53
manna, 76-78, 79
Mary, 65
Matthew, Gospel of, 41, 43, 84, 96, 98